ZOOM
School

Reptiles

Desert Tortoises

by Elizabeth Thomas

Consulting Editor: Gail Saunders-Smith, PhD

Content Consultant: Tanya Dewey, PhD
University of Michigan Museum of Zoology

CAPSTONE PRESS
a capstone imprint

Pebble Plus is published by Capstone Press,
1710 Roe Crest Drive, North Mankato, Minnesota 56003.
www.capstonepub.com

 Books published by Capstone Press are manufactured with paper
containing at least 10 percent post-consumer waste.

Library of Congress Cataloging-in-Publication Data
Thomas, Elizabeth, 1953–
  Desert tortoises / by Elizabeth Thomas.
    p. cm.—(Pebble plus. Reptiles.)
  Includes bibliographical references and index.
  Summary: "Simple text and photographs present desert tortoises, how they look, where they live, and what
they do"—Provided by publisher.
  ISBN 978-1-4296-6645-9 (library binding)
  1. Desert tortoise—Juvenile literature. I. Title.
  QL666.C584T46 2012
  597.92'4—dc22

                        2011002110

Editorial Credits
Lori Shores, editor; Gene Bentdahl, designer; Laura Manthe, production specialist

Photo Credits
© Dwight Kuhn Photography/David Kuhn, 5, 9; Alamy: Kevin Ebi, 15; CORBIS: Kennan Ward, 19; Dreamstime:
Jacysworld, 7, Mesquite53, front cover; fotolia: PixyNL, back cover; iStockphoto: leosgnarly, 1; KimballStock: Tom & Pat
Leeson; Minden Pictures: ZSSD, 11; Photo Researchers, Inc: William H. Mullins, 13

Note to Parents and Teachers

The Reptiles set supports science standards related to life science. This book describes and
illustrates desert tortoises. The images support early readers in understanding the text. The
repetition of words and phrases helps early readers learn new words. This book also introduces
early readers to subject-specific vocabulary words, which are defined in the Glossary section.
Early readers may need assistance to read some words and to use the Table of Contents,
Glossary, Read More, Internet Sites, and Index sections of the book.

Printed in the United States of America in North Mankato, Minnesota.
042014
008100R

Table of Contents

Land Turtles

Some turtles have webbed
feet for swimming.
But desert tortoises have
round feet for walking.
They only live on land.

Up Close!

Desert tortoises weigh
24 to 50 pounds
(11 to 23 kilograms).
They have greenish-tan
to dark brown shells.

Desert tortoises have
thick legs that look like
tiny elephant legs.
Claws on their front feet
help them dig.

Hot and Dry Homes

Desert tortoises live in grassy, sandy, and rocky desert areas. They live only in northern Mexico and the southwestern United States.

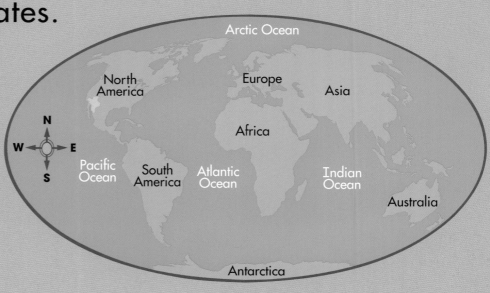

where desert tortoises live

Desert tortoises dig
burrows to live in.
The burrows stay cool
in the hot day
and warm at night.

Rain rarely falls
in the desert.
Desert tortoises get water
by eating grasses,
wildflowers, and cactuses.

From Egg to Tortoise

Female desert tortoises
lay eggs when they are
15 to 20 years old.
The eggs are the size
of Ping-Pong balls.

Desert Tortoise Life Cycle

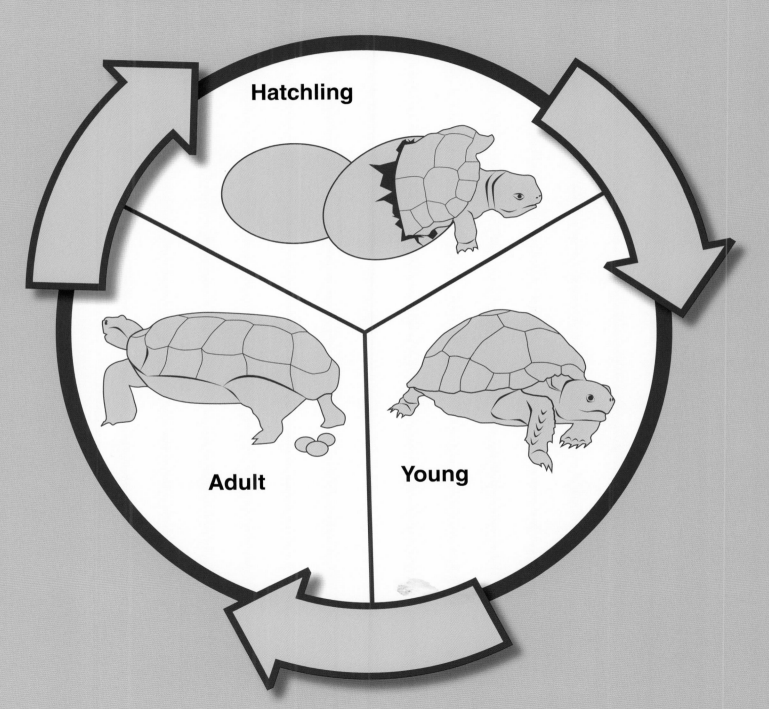

Hatchling

Adult

Young

Young tortoises hatch after 90 to 135 days. They look for food and dig burrows right away. Desert tortoises live up to 100 years.

Saving the Desert Tortoise

Desert tortoises are
in danger of dying out.
Laws protect these animals
and the areas where they live.

Glossary

burrow—a tunnel or hole in the ground made or used by an animal

cactus—a plant covered in spines that is found in desert areas

claw—a hard curved nail on the foot of an animal

desert—a dry area with little rain

hatch—to break out of an egg

protect—to guard or keep safe from harm

webbed—having folded skin or tissue between an animal's toes or fingers

Read More

Dickmann, Nancy. *A Turtle's Life.* Watch It Grow. Chicago: Heinemann Library, 2011.

Shaskan, Trisha Speed. *What's the Difference Between a Turtle and a Tortoise?* What's the Difference? Mankato, Minn.: Picture Window Books, 2011.

Underwood, Gary. *Reptiles.* Weird, Wild, and Wonderful. New York: Gareth Stevens Pub., 2010.

Internet Sites

FactHound offers a safe, fun way to find Internet sites related to this book. All of the sites on FactHound have been researched by our staff.

Here's all you do:

Visit *www.facthound.com*

Type in this code: 9781429666459

Check out projects, games and lots more at
www.capstonekids.com

Index

Word Count: 176
Grade: 1
Early-Intervention Level: I